Thoughts from a Renaissance Man

by

Kevin Ross Emery

Being and becoming the most you can be in any lifetime has always been my goal. Being a Renaissance Man is integral part of that process.

Table of Contents

To My Newborn Nephew	6
Rosalie	7
L'Chiem	8
A Prayer for You	9
Just	10
The Journey Home	11
The Journey Back	13
A Tree in Winter	15
Kitten in my Pocket	16
The Other Woman	18
Afternoon Tea	19
Laus	20
The Sailors	21
An Afternoon Well Spent	22
Through New Eyes	23
And I Will Return	24
Life	25
Time Passages	26
And More Time Passes	27
Marion	28
To Jamie	29
At Last	30
Missing Michelle	31
Autumn Dawn	32
More	33
To Rodger	34
Better Than Nothing	35
Mother	36
Today	37
Brass Ring	38
My Eyes	39
Tug of War	41
Camping	42
Veils	44
My Papa	45

Child of Innocence	46
Old Stand-bys	47
Waiting to Grow Up	48
Childless	49
Papa's Hands	50
Watch	51
Cocoon	53
Papa's Illness	54
Winter	55
Come with Me	56
Papa's Pill Box	57
Winter Solstice	58
Paper Cuts	59
Words of Love	60
David Lee	61
Pent-up	62
You Promised Not to Go	63
Faith	65
Rain	66
Fire in the Morning	67
For Cousin Michael	68
Sea Children	69
For Laura	70
Seventeen	71
For Mary Mitchell	72
Spring Cleaning	73
Fully	74
Still	75
Happy 25th Alicia	76
Sunshine	77
If Only	78
In a Million Years	79
The Death of a Million Years	80
The Fool	81
Jacqui's Story	82

To My New-Born Nephew

If I could only see through your eyes,
    Discovering everything new,
Seeing everything as it is,
    Through the purity of innocence.

Look good and remember well,
    How things truly are,
Before they become distorted,
    Through judgmental eyes.

Before you learn of right & wrong,
    Beautiful & ugly,
See everything for the beauty,
    In just the fact of its being.

1981

Rosalie

Swishing and swaying,
   With beauty and grace
      Laughing at all things,
         In the kindest of ways.

      Never existing,
         Always living,
            Laughing and living
               You are many things to many people.

         You are always passing gifts,
            Gifts of laughter,
             Gifts of warmth,
                But mostly gifts of love.

L'Chiem

Somewhere along the way,
    I forget what it was to be alive.
Getting so caught in the necessities of living,
    That I had begun but to function.

There are many deaths,
    One may experience
And survive,
    Within the processes of life.

The loss of the feeling,
    Of what it is to be alive.
Perhaps the most common,
    Also most reconcilable, if you have not forgotten how.

I think I shall choose to be alive again,
    While the memory is still vivid.
And the taste still lingers in my mouth,
    Like the taste of peanuts.

A Prayer for You

I send a prayer for you,
    Every night,
That everyday you will awake,
    And see the grass is a little greener,
Just because you are alive.

And I pray for you every night,
    That the joy that lies within your soul,
Will surface to your consciousness,
    And flood you,
With its intensity.

And before I end each prayer, I send for you,
    I ask that you shall awake,
And see all the wonderful and special things,
    We know you are,
We being, God & me.

Just

The wind blew today,
    -just to clean the air.
The clouds rained today,
    -just to clean the earth.
I cried today,
    -just to clean the soul.
And there was a rainbow today,
    -just to give me hope.

1974

The Journey Home

Last call, Flight 1426 boomed,
    It shook me into reality,
As I boarded quickly,
    For the journey home.

Papa would be waiting at the gate,
    An many others waited- elsewhere,
Friends and family, to touch me,
    To be touched by me.

And the questions waited,
    Why did I not come back,
What kept me there,
    The shakiness of my career or failure of my marriage.

With love & caring,
    They all wanted to know,
They all wanted me back,
    Few knew how much I changed.

Last time I saw most of them,
    They were dancing at my wedding,
Last time I talked to most of them,
    They were crying at my loss.

Thirty pounds lighter,
    Mentally and emotionally,
Many years older,
    Was I ready for the journey home.

The flight descended,
    My spirits ascended,
Perhaps here were the missing pieces,
    Of who I was and what I am.

How many tears would fall?
        How many of them mine.
What realizations would come,
        On the journey home.

I grab my bag,
        Straighten my shoulders,
Breath deep,
        And go to find out.

1990

The Journey Back

Flight 1425, last call,
    I moved to the gate,
Boarding I was prepared,
    For the journey back.

I knew much waited for me,
    At the place I now call home,
Things that kept my life going,
    Or what I now call my life.

The life that I had left behind,
    Was no longer mine,
And the life I was going back to was merely a shadow,
    Of what my life had been.

I knew when my world went spiraling,
    Out of control,
There was no going home,
    Till I gained control.

Moving away,
    Had not been running away,
But going back,
    At this point would have been.

But resolving as many issues,
    As it is my power to resolve,
Dealing with as much pain and hurt, As I need to,
    Was it time to go home?

Integrate,
    All I wanted to keep from my marriage,
Discarding,
    All the baggage I wanted to lose.

Emerging,
    As the person I was now,
And learning,
    To love that person all over again.

These were my goals,
    I was doing well towards reaching them,
Would going home facilitate them,
    Or enable me to stagnate - to backslide?

The plane has landed,
    My thoughts are still in flight, though,
No decisions made yet,
    On the journey back.

1990

A Tree in Winter

Empty arms reaching for the sun,
        Black against white snow,
Cracking more as each day is done.
        With each breeze feeling with songs of woe.

Once it was a leafy green,
        Then it came to full color on an autumn day.
In it once life could be seen.
        Now all life has gone away.

But it is really not sapped of all life.
        For soon it will bud.
Being the sun's wife,
        When frozen ground turns to mud.

But Spring is still so far away,
        It has now only the cold,
Which stays with it all the day.
        Aging it, sapping it youth-make it grow old.

Kitten in My Pocket

You've heard,
>I suppose,
Of the Cat
>In the Hat.

I have a different tail,
>To tell,
For its no cat in a hat,
>For me - you see.

For me,
>It's my kitten,
Sitting in my pocket,
>Which is my tail to tell.

A little black head,
>All purr, fur and paws,
Riding in style,
>Upon my hip.

Like a princess,
>Swathed in royal red,
Or at the very least the royal red,
>Of my old terrycloth dressing gown.

Disdainfully she rides,
>Looking down.
At her subjects,
>From high up upon my hips.

The dogs may whine,
>Mr. Ferret, poke to be noticed,
But for my money,
>And my heart too.
It will still always be,
>My kitten,

Sitting in my pocket,
   Which does it for me.

The Other Woman

Listen to me, lady of mystique,
      For I have seen your beauty is beyond skin deep.
As I have seen your soul, flashing in your eyes.
      Aren't you sick, other woman, of living other's lies?

You are their fantasies, so tempting, so cool.
      But haven't you learned that part is always love's fool.
For one never gives his soul to a fantasy,
      So why not come and be my reality.

Afternoon Tea

Sometimes I still crave,
    Afternoon teas,
Laced with Sonatas,
    And fine china.

Have proper tea,
    With me.
Civilized conversation,
    White gloves and cookies.

Let us discuss,
    Moliere and Voltaire,
In straight back chairs,
    In front of a fireplace.

Permeate the air,
    With fresh flowers,
And burning logs,
    All lit by candlelight.

Let the music,
    Sing to me,
Of proper romance,
    Laced with shy glances.

Take from me,
    Discussions that are punctuated with profanity,
And ungracious innuendo by people,
    Who think of the classics as television shows.

1989

Laus

Running and diving through the waves,
    You become exhilarated,
As your skin tingles
    And you shiver from the cold.

You come back
    Throwing yourself onto hot sands,
Worshipping the sun
    As others walking by worship you.

1986

The Sailor

The winds have filled the sails
      And the smell of the ocean euphorically filled my head.
The boat has journey of at least another day,
      Before she reaches home.
As for me, I am home
      And my soul well anchored where she belongs.

1984

An Afternoon Well Spent

Spring, sprung,
    A heat wave hit.
Carrots cut, celery sliced,
    There is a picnic in the air.

A cooler of Coors Light,
    And a kite,
And old friend found,
    A day which makes memories.

Down dirt roads,
    The car left behind,
Bouncing over barbed wire and barreling through cockaburs,
    War wounds speak of our victories.

An afternoon well spent,
    Batoid flew,
Cards were dealt, rocks were climbed,
    And rivers were crossed.

Clouds came,
    Goosebumps grew,
Time to go,
    No regrets.

Plans, planned,
    Promises and proposals,
Of time to be spent together,
    An afternoon well spent.

Through New Eyes

Engulfed,
    With so many feelings,
Good and bad,
    It is as if my soul is floating.

And through so much,
    Release,
Of old albatrosses,
    I have found my wings.

And with new wings, have come new eyes.
    As I feel as if I am seeing,
So many things for the first time.
    Becoming over-loaded with emotions.

So good,
    To be,
So totally,
    Alive.

1983

And I Will Return

I have hurt you,
    My friend,
Though no thought,
    Was further from my mind.

And as I move forward,
    Evolving each day,
Deeper into myself,
    I leave you behind.

But some things,
    One must do alone,
One can only do alone,
    And it is my time alone.

But stay my friend,
    My friend,
And gladly will I share,
    All I have learned,
When I return.

1987

Life

I watched a new leaf,
    Break from a tree,
Then I saw the new leaf,
    Whipped by the wind across the sky.
And I watched the rain,
    Batter it to the ground.
Looking at the leaf,
    I cried.
But wiping my eyes,
    I chose to ride the wind,
And feel the rain,
    For it was better than dying on a branch.

Time Passages

How can I be,
        One year older,
Through but the passing of a hand,
        From one side of midnight to the other.

Was not this year,
        Passed through moments,
Moments which made memories,
        Good and bad.

And can I be the same type,
        Of year older,
As I was through the last passing,
        Of this event.

I think not,
        Perhaps ten years passed,
This year,
        Perhaps not.

And it will only be,
        When the journey has finished,
And the total distance looked at,
        That I will know how much was passed,
In the last year.

4 July 1987

And More Time Passes

And another Christmas passes,
    Just as another Thanksgiving is gone.
But there was no last-minute gift making,
    Nor drumstick saved,
At least not for you.

As each holiday passes,
    The last one you were here is a little farther away.
I keep thinking it will be easier,
    But you flood my thoughts
And live on through all our memories.

Eight years ago, last Christmas you were here,
    Eight years ago, last Easter you were gone,
I miss you as much now as I did then,
    We all do.

But how clear our memories are of you,
    Your last-minute present making,
Your love of "A Christmas Carol",
    And the eating of the drumstick,

We smile,
    Happy for all we did share,
Even as we cry for all that,
    You did not.

Marion

Click of your heels,
        Click of your tongue,
Quick with your wit,
        And eyes full of fun.

Snappy retorts,
        And, That's not my job!
Said with a wicked grin,
        A smile and a sob.

You keep then in line,
        Letting then think that their boss,
Yet the truth is evident,
        As walk away giving your head that certain toss.

To Jaime

We fly a kite,
      Jog a block,
You learn a new word from me,
      And I tie your red velvet hair ribbons.

You're my little girl,
      You will have a place with me,
Both in my heart & my life,
      Always.

And though I have other nieces and other nephews,
      And also have a place for them,
Never forget my little Jamie,
      There is always that place just for you.

1987

At Last (for John G.)

You,
        Born old,
                Old & cynical,
                      Afraid of yourself, and the world.

I am watching you,
        Growing up,
Growing young,
        Less cynical as you finally,
Fall in love.

Missing Michele

Nothing seems quite right,
      And yet nothing is really wrong.
I can't quite put a finger on it,
      But I know it is there.

The world is safe,
      These days,
At least my world,
      It's still a crazy world,
But that is my world.

Everything is running smoothly,
      At least as smoothly,
As it ever does,
      But something is just not right.

I wish you were here,
      To discuss it with,
To tell me what you think.

1987

Autumn Dawn

Raspberry sherbet,
      In a blueberry sky,
Glowing through ancient fingers,
      Who in fragility, reach for the sky?

Fall all but gone,
      Winter all but here.
Morning windows,
      Sparkle a milk-glazed surface.

People scuttle,
      Watching their breaths.
Running from the cold,
      Running to keep warm.

No leaves,
      No snow,
Fall all but gone,
      Winter all but here.

1978

More

I know you'll be here tomorrow,
      But not for all my tomorrows.
Like you were here yesterday,
      But not for all my yesterdays.

I was,
      Before you.
I will be,
      After you, but,
I will be more,
      Because of you.

To Rodger

Walking through the myst of time
Mysterious and melancholy
Knowingly toward the pre-ordained fate
Of an early demise

Chanting the doxology
Of fate and acceptance
Passing through the paradoxical halls
Of mausoleum and museum

Silent screams
Unshed tears
Torn between the acceptance
And the human desire to survive

Seemingly serene
A facade for fear
From which intensely flows
Messages from the gods

Through words and pictures
Visions and verbiage
A mighty messenger
Who dwells but too briefly
With us here.

July 5, 1996

Better Than Nothing

Huddled within my sheets,
    I am wrapped in the pain,
That lies between my sheets,
    At least I am not between the sheets alone.

Giving of myself,
    & if my love,
I reap the rewards,
    Of pain and memories.

But at least,
    Laying alone,
I am not alone,
    For I always have the pain.

And the pain I have,
    Compares nothing to the emptiness,
I would have experienced,
    If I had experienced nothing.

Mother

Slowly I come to discover you,
As if seeing you for the very first time.
You step off a pedestal,
Made of love and hate,
To become human.

I see you now,
For both your frailties,
And your strengths.
I see you now,
As a person.

A person,
With whom I have spent,
My whole life with,
And yet never looked at,
As a person.

A warm-hearted woman,
With insecurities and unsurities
Of fifty years.
Special, in her own way,
Is my mother.

1986

Today

We are only shadowy images
      Whom are elusively playing hide & seek.
I am yesterday,
      You are tomorrow,
And we are but a brief moment
      -called today.

1977

Brass Ring

Sometimes I want it all.
        And it seems as if
I cannot get it fast enough.
        I feel as if I am on a carousel.

I am on a carousel.
        Reaching for the brass ring.
And the faster I run to get it,
        The faster it moves.
I run faster and faster,
        Until everything blurs
As it is moving faster and faster, too.

Everything stops.
        There is no brass ring.
Someone has taken my brass ring.
        And I lay down
And I cry..

1976

My Eyes

I could but give to you,
    My glasses, my vision, my sight,
So that you just might,
    See yourself through my eyes.

Proud and strong,
    (Occasionally even head strong),
You have so much to give,
    And get so caught in giving that you question.

You question do I give,
    Too much,
Too little,
    The question is for whom do you ask the question?

You give what you need to give,
    Demand what you need to take,
If they want more, perhaps it is not you who they want,
    But just anyone to feed their bottomless pit of need.

And if they cannot give to you what you need,
    Whether it be friend or lover,
Then perhaps you need to walk alone with no shattered expectations,
    Or walk with someone who cares enough about your needs to want to fulfill them.

Be confident and brave,
    My little friend,
For if you could see yourself through my eyes,
    Let me tell you what you would see.

You would see more love than any one person could deserve to get,
    In one lifetime.
A caring that is gentle, yet strong.

A mind that is open to growth,
And a heart that is expandable beyond belief.

You would see warm humor,
    That pours out of an open mind,
And a giving heart,
    Laced with caring and sharing.

Truth which is not delivered to you,
    Like a billy club,
But handed to you,
    Like a cane.

See all of these things and then you will know:
    You deserve all that you demand,
And you will demand all that you deserve,
    Come see yourself through my eyes, my friend.

        1986

Tug of War

I pull back,
        You push forward.
I feel uncomfortable,
        You comfort me.

I fight for control,
        You fight back.
It is a tug of war,
        The prize: my life.

We want the same thing,
        To see me happy,
For me to have what is best,
        Or at least what is best for me.

But it is my life,
        Yet the tug of war continues,
And I stop to wonder,
        Do all mothers & sons play such games,
With so much at stake.

Whose life is it?
        Time will have the answer.

1979

Camping

Remember going camping,
    Must been 'bout eight,
Papa, Aunt Glennice, my brother Bobby, cousin Nicky, and me,
    We couldn't wait.

Traveled international,
    Tell you that's what we did,
Up into Quebec,
    That is where we hid.

Now being youngest of the lot,
    No one asked me nothing,
And nothings what they got.
    Which is too bad cause they needed all the help they could get.

Papa and Aunt Glennice,
    Said many a things,
That only adults could say,
    They wrestled with those tent poles about half the day.

Up it went,
    And down again,
Before we could get inside,
    Us kids tried to help but the giggles got in the way.

We laughed, we played,
    We got, we gave,
Ordered us some French toast in a restaurant,
    That was as close as any of us had been to France!

Then packed we did,
    Decided to take a chance.
For those French sparkles, were just too good to pass,
    But how to sneak them cross the border without the guard's harass?

Aunt Glennice had the thought,
      Which turn to save the day,
To stick'em down her shirt, hiding them that way.
      Papa said "Good idea, you don't have nothing there anyway.
She glared at him,
      While she was putting them down,
She gave him the finger,
      Told him he was a clown.

So we sweat it out,
      Looking as innocent as we could,
Our '69 version of being from the hood.
      The guard peered in saying "howdy Mam"
We hardly breathed until he waved us away
      Aunt Glennice said "Hit it brother, drive as fast as you can."

The sparklers have long been gone,
      Not the only ones to go,
Aunt Glennice went, my brother Bobby too,
      Now Papa has joined them at the place where sparkles burn all the time.

Now there is only cousin Nick and I
      And the laughter that we share
When we remember going camping,
      To the land up over there.

Veils

Let me pull a veil,
    See what I have found,
I have found a layer of fear,
    Fear that is abound.

Here comes another veil,
    Now what shall I see,
It is a layer of loneliness,
    That lay before me.

On another veil,
    I shall drop the pin,
I see lurking some doubt,
    Doubt that lies within.

Here comes another veil,
    Now what do I spy,
It is warmth laced with humor,
    Before my very eyes.

Digging yet deeper, through another veil,
    I see some charm and wit,
Intermingled with the warmth,
    Just for the hell of it.

Beating still,
    Under another veil,
A good and warm heart,
    And an ego that is frail.

I those twinkling eyes I see,
    Beating in your soul,
Beneath all those veils is just you,
    So much more precious than gold.

My Papa

Papa.
      My Papa.
Where have you gone?
      When did you slip away?

I see you there,
      I see the body,
A body that was supposed to have been dead,
      So long ago,

The body remains,
      But what happened to my Papa?
Who stole him away, into the vague looks, the repeated questions.
      What happened to the sharp mind that I loved so well,
That loved me so well?

My rock, my strength, the insights I could always count on,
      Where have they gone?
What thief could be so cruel,
      To have stolen my Papa and left me with this fraud?
This impersonator? This body, whose mind I can only in vague moments and glittering exceptions see my Papa.
      Oh Papa where have you gone?
Are you happy there?
      For I am not happy here without you.

Tuesday, May 09, 2006

Child of Innocence

Can you not come play with me?
        Come play with me,
In the sunshine,
        Be a child with me.

Is it not possible,
        To regain innocence?
Is it that innocence so lost,
        Or are we just so removed we cannot see it?

Does everything have to have a purpose?
        But if being happy is not my purpose,
(Is it not yours?)
        And being a child is happiness,
Then does it not have a purpose?
        Come, be a child with me.

1976

Old Stand-bys…like forever

Beyond original innocence's,
      Past the nativity,
Of youth,
      Yet not old.

And even though,
      That certain innocence's,
Found in adult youths is gone,
      Disillusionment has not arrived,
Nor I am sure it ever will.

I can never see me,
      Indifferent to a rainbow,
Unmoved to a love song,
      Or giving up on forever's.

1985

Waiting to Grow Up

What to do, what to be,
    When I grew up,
I would just have to wait and see,
    What I have and not I know.

I remember wanting to be:
    Like Ben Franklin,
One week,
    Like Al Capone,
The next.
    But too hard, I thought, to be like them,
I'll just be me,
    Then I learned, too hard sometimes,
Just to be me.

Already twenty-six,
    Still I am clueless,
On what a fix.

Almost twenty-seven,
    "Time to decide,
        Time to decide, Kevin"

What to do,
    What to be,
When I grow-up,
    Just have to wait and see,
Maybe growing-up,
    Is just not for me.

Child-Less

Tears held back,
    As I face a world,
From which you may go.
    You, who knew me, before I knew what it was to know.

I, not having lost you, yet,
    Knowing that soon I might.
Cannot face a world,
    Without you in my sight..

And as I think,
    Papa do not go,
Feeling three, not thirty-three,
    Child-less, I wonder when It is my time will anybody be there for me.

Papa's Hands

Your hands,
    Held me,
When I was still small enough,
    To be held by two hands.

Firm and fleshy hands,
    Knuckles of a boxer,
Heart of a father,
    Those are Papa's hands.

Hands that sponged my brow,
    When high fevers grasped me,
Death threatened me,
    But you fought and won me.

Hands that lifted me,
    Until I was too big,
With arms that hugged me,
    (For which you are never too old.)

Hands that grasped my shoulders,
    And held me,
When the world turned against me,
    Those were Papa's hands.

Papa's hands,
    That landscaped the beauty,
And built the fences,
    Tough hands full of love,

Full of love,
    Full of compassion and beauty,
Life has been full for me,
    Helped with Papa's hands.

Watch

Ambient light,
    Ambient noise
Looking at my reflection,
    Huddled over the keyboard,
Sitting in a room with a view.

I always wanted a corner office,
    Over-looking a teeming metropolis,
Looking down from one of the highest buildings in town.

In my wildest dreams,
    I never thought of the way in which,
My dream would come true.
    Wrong town, wrong place and yet hear I sit,
    Sitting looking out of the three-quarter length, glass windows
Listening not to the hum of the business machines but typing to the dulcet tones
    Of life and death machines, punctuated by the grasping breaths of my father.

"Doing a death watch"
    My father puts it,
In between struggling breaths.
    I ask him why.
He tells me he's too tired, too much pain.
    It has all just become too much.

But then I remember all the times,
    They told me,
He had not six months to live,
    Now that was over twenty years ago.
Making one of the things I love about Papa,
    He gets more out of six months than anyone I know.

Then there was he would not make the week,

On his last legs and failing fast.
Ah but, my father the thief,
    Always one to cheat death,
Stole a new pair of legs and has been on them ten years hence.

Then there was the doc who said,
    "Go home, climb in bed and wait to be dead,
Papa told him he would die,
    When he was god dam good and ready
"And I will probably out live you." He added for good measure.

The doc is dead now,
    He died six months later,
Perhaps that is where Papa got the new legs,
    So many years ago, after all the doc did not need them anymore.

Or perhaps it is different now, one cannot tell,
    For before it was always someone else,
Telling Papa that he was going to die,
    And him telling them to go to hell.

But if he says it,
    If he proclaims it is his death watch,
Then has he truly run the course and is he headed for home?
    Who knows.

But for now,
    I sit in my corner office,
With three quarter length windows,
    In one of the tallest buildings in town.
To the backdrop of Papa's struggling breaths, each one,
    Like the tick of a watch winding down.

Cocoon

Quietly I contemplate all that is said,
    You say I do not hear,
And yet I have never stopped listening,
    I just need time.

Leave me
    For now,
Within my cocoon,
    Digesting all I have heard and know.

And let me reassure you,
    That I know that you care,
For you would not be here now,
    If you did not.

Papa's Illness

Flowing through,
    Towards a blocked passage,
It creates new passages,
    Temporarily.

Trying to fix it,
    Might kill you quickly,
To not,
    Will kill you slowly.

You are not ready to go,
    I am not ready to let you.
Or maybe it is not you that is not ready,
    Perhaps it is just me, who is not ready,
Don't go.

Winter

Winter,
      Drifting again,
Upon my realities,
      Like drifting snow.

Oh so many winters
      Have come and gone,
They have passed through me,
      On the hills of Vermont
And roared up to me,
      On the coast of Maine, ah Winter.

It is winter again,
      I look and see the endless whiteness,
Winds,
      Which never completely stop.

I lean back,
      Squinting at the Winter's sun,
And smile to myself,
      As I reach for my glass.

Winter has never been better,
      As I stop and sip fruity delights,
Winter could never be better than this one,
      Perched on a Caribbean beach, on the endless white sand.

Come with Me

In crystal blue skies,
    Walk with me,
In new spring woods,
    Travel with me.

Along a running brook,
    Wait with me for Spring,
Stand with me and hold my hand.
    Breath with me the crisp clean air.
Share with me all my life,
    Come live with me,
And be my wife.

Papa's Pill Box

I will always remember,
    Papa's pill box,
It was small and round,
    Like a pocket watch.

It had a little button,
    On one of its sides,
Which when you push,
    Shows, what it hides.

Bright blue on the front,
    The center inlaid,
With a star-burst pattern,
    All which has begun to fade.

Inside held three white triangles,
    And in each a different color pill,
Pretty maybe, but never did I touch.
    Because to me they might kill.

Now as I am older,
    It holds no great mystery,
But treasure it I always will,
    For it is part of Papa's history.

And the day will come,
    No matter how much I dread,
When all I shall have of Papa,
    Will be his pill box, and all the things he said.

Winter Solstice

In frozen stillness,
    Brushed with white,
It was a mixture of nature and man,
    That lined the sky.

Telephone poles laced with crochet cotton sparkled,
    Lighted by the rising sun,
And back dropped,
    By an explosion of colors.

The air, cold & crisp,
    Was the kind that made you want to run,
To celebrate,
    To live.

The glimmering lights played tag,
    On an almost frozen marsh.
The smell of the salt water exhilarated my senses,
    It was good to be home.

1982

Papercuts

Papercuts,
    From letters in the mail,
A farewell from a friend,
    Which makes me grow pale.

Oh how a letter,
    Can cut like a knife,
When the envelope is filled with a note,
    That ends the togetherness that was our life.

It is the deepness of the friendship,
    That deepens the wounds,
It was supposed to be our friendship,
    Yet you alone called the end to the tune.

Clear, yet blood filled tears,
    Fall from my eyes,
As you wrench from my heart that which was ours,
    With your self-imposed good-byes.

You can remove the tomorrow,
    In which our friendship would have grown,
But the years of our past shall haunt you,
    When at the end of it all you remember the last seed you had sown.

And when the time comes to look back,
    And think of what we have to regret,
When it comes to us, I shall have none, and will speak fondly, always,
    Of all that we had and the day that we met.

Words of Love

Never for you,
        Do the right words,
Fall from my lips,
        No matter how I try.

Funny I, who write words of love,
        To you, whom I love the most,
Somehow just seem to stutter like a child,
        Just learning to speak.

Perhaps I try,
        Too hard to tell you,
How much I love you,
        If I only knew that you knew,
I would not have to try so much.

David Lee

Bright green eyes,
        And auburn hair.
Braces faced with green,
        Energy to spare.

Such dreams,
        Young man,
Visions of books you've written,
        Lots of fans.

Millions of thoughts,
        Even more words,
Stories to tell,
        Some sci-fi others comedy absurd.

So write every day,
        Find something to say,
Work daily at your craft,
        And your well on your way.

Keep your sparkle,
        Glowing in your eyes,
Focus your mind,
        And onto paper put your daydreaming sighs.

I learn back in my chair,
        And picture this is for you,
David Lee, best-selling author,
        Believe it, it can be true.

Pent-Up

Is it so wrong for me to be angry?
      Am I not allowed the feeling,
The feeling of hate,
      Just because I love?

May I not yell and scream of the injustice of it all,
      Must I hold it all in,
Until I am ready to cry from the pain,
      And then not be allowed to cry from either?

You Promised Not to Go

You promised not to go,
    Before.
He went before.
    And it almost killed her.

He went before,
    His father and his mother,
Before his sister and his brothers,
    He went to early and none of our lives were the same.

You told me you would stay,
    We shared the horror and the heartache of his death.
The tears that we thought mother would never stop crying,
    We lived through the pain that seemed to never go away.

You promised to wait,
    No early death for you.
No leaving me, as mother's last one standing.
    I was happy being the baby.

Fir you see,
    When Billy went, you were now the oldest,
So to speak,
    But me, I was still the baby.

He died in Spring, on Easter,
    Easter would never be the same.
You died in Spring,
    Giving us all a Memorial Day we will never forget.

Perhaps you thought twenty-seven years,
    Was enough,
Enough that we were all older and stronger now.
    But you leave behind the wife, the kids,
The reminders he never did.

But twenty-seven was not enough,
    Not enough by far,
Not talking to you much of late, never thinking
    That I would never talk to you again.

You promised,
    Not while Mother was alive,
I always suspected I would be the last man standing,
    But not this way, never this way.
I miss you more than you would have ever thought,
    For there are no bigger brothers now,
No one who remembers like you did,
    All that we went through;
Different fathers, different friends but we three always had each other and now
    There is only one.

The hurt is different but just as deep,
    I only smile when I realize that the two of you together,
Get to guide me, from above,
    Me, the last man standing.

26 November 2006

Faith

Cloistered within,
    Your up-bringing
Entwined and ensnared
    In values taught to you your whole life.

So ready to give,
    So much to give,
But all so conditional,
    It limits the rewards you can reap.

If you could but give,
    Knowing it is a gift,
A gift from a loving God,
    Instead of holding back
In fear of your wrathful God,
    What changes it would make.

With the truest beauty,
    Of a rose,
I wonder if you'll ever bloom,
    Or die without opening
Wasting and missing so much.

Rain

Wandering in the rain
        I feel it upon my skin,
As it seeps through my clothes,
        And care not of what I wear.

It is most important,
        That feet,
Inhale it,
        Smell it
Taste it
        Absorb it,

For it reminds me that I live.

Fire in the Morning

Burning embers,
    Glowing silently,
In the early morning dew,
    Waiting for the first shaft of light.

Holding my breath,
    One breaks free,
Literally running up the side,
    Of the slumbering mountain.

Ablaze,
    With brilliantly glistening,
Reds, oranges, yellows and purples,
    Back dropped by Evergreens,
I sigh.

The morning screeches,
    Like a bird,
With color now,
    My breath and the morning mist mingle.

Adding to the luminous lightshow,
    Provided by Mother,
Each and every day unique,
    When fall comes to New England.

    18 October 2006

For Cousin Michael

I reach for you,
  You are distant,
I try to jog your memory,
  Of the closeness we once had,
Your silence feigns knowledge of such a bond.

You were always,
  My favorite cousin,
And although spoiled and rotten,
  I loved you,
As one of my youthful best friends.

We shared dreams & Secrets,
  Playing games,
Only understood by little boys,
  Picking on your little sister and cousin Kelly,
When you were with me, we shared everything.

Now we share nothing,
  You politely ask me about my life,
I tell you as you listen but do not hear.
  And when I ask about you,
I get cryptic answers.

Strangers now,
  It hurts,
As time passes, I will accept your distance,
  But as long as I see you and remember,
It will hurt.

Sea Children

Children,
      Diving through the waves,
With squeals of laughter & surprise,
      At the coldness of the water.

Children,
      Who splash, taunt, & tease each other,
And themselves,
      With each new wave.

Children,
      From six,
To sixty,
      But all are children.

And I am one of them.

1987

For Laura

When I see Iris's
    I think of you,
Images of your smile,
       Flood my mind.

There almost pushy purple,
       Conjure up the hats you wore,
The way they sway,
       The way you dance.

The impertinent way,
       They dominate any place they grow,
Brings memories of our escapades,
       Complete with coffee and more sunrises than I can count.

When I think of you,
    My love,
I see Irises,
    No roses for you, my love.
Only Irises.

Seventeen

Tis hell to be but seventeen,
        Too old to be cute,
Too young to be anything else.
        Stuck within obscurity,
Not quite an adult,
        (Too old for a child.)

You're stuck between
        Knowing nothing,
And yet knowing better.
        Love is to be unimportant
And yet it's your whole world.
        They say you know nothing of the world
But you know of heartache, pain, love and joy.
        What else is there to know?

They can't tell you what,
        You'll just have to wait and see,
Tis hell to be but seventeen.

1977

For Mary Mitchell

Angelic looks,
      And devilish laughs,
Sweet sounds of song pour out, as well as,
      Salty stories.

Such a mixture,
      My mistress Mary, mine.
From her Catholic comments,
      To her invitations to mayhem.

My little Mary Sunshine.

Always keeping me on my toes,
      And yet sometimes I think I know what no one else knows,
That little Mistress Mary Sunshine.
      Is truly all these things and more.

Spring Cleaning

It smells musky,
>It is time,
For spring cleaning,
>To begin.

To open the windows,
>Blow out,
The cobwebs,
>Freshen up the air.

Much to: revitalize
  clean,
>scrub,
Or just throw out.

What lies under,
>-the cobwebs.
And what lies behind,
>-the doors.

Time to find out,
>Need a strong wind,
Perhaps even a good rain,
>For it is time to do some spring cleaning,
- in my life.

Fully

I crave elegance,
        I want wings
Fly me to the moon,
        Help me shine like the sun.

Roaring, as do the crashing waves,
        I wander aimlessly,
Singing half melodies.
        But doing so whole heartedly

And is it not better to sing,
        Half a song - whole heartedly,
Than a whole song,
        Half-heartedly?

September 1, 1999

Still

Years have passed,
    But my thoughts of you have not.
Still I feel you here with me,
    Laughing at me, and with me,
Telling me how you feel,
    As you always did,
Without saying anything at all.

And though you have died, you will never go away,
    Not for me you won't,
Nor will you for the others that have known and loved you,
    You gave too much,
You have meant too much to ever really be gone.

Years have passed, but not the feelings,
    At least the special ones,
It does hurt less, but that came in time.
    The time it took me to realize that your death did not mean you were gone.

But the feelings,
    The special ones,
Are with me still,
    As you are.

For my brother: William Daniel Emery
1985

Happy 25th Alicia

A year older,
  A year longer that I have known you,
A year in which you've grown ten,
  A year that has brought us closer than we have ever been.

A year of looking back,
  A year of letting go,
A year of grabbing on,
  A year of moving forward.

Next year for you I wish:

Twice as much growth,
  Half as much pain,
To grow stronger, If possible,
  And someone to see and love you, for who you are.

Sunshine

Let me tell you about the sunshine,
    It's always somewhere,
Sometimes it's on the other side of the world,
    But it's there.

I think of that thought often,
    Around midnight,
When it seems the darkest and coldest,
    That there is sunshine somewhere.

And even though,
    It is on the other side,
Of the world,
    I know it's coming back.

I hold that thought,
    Close to me,
When I know I need the warmth and light,
    Of the sunshine, most.

So, when its coldest and darkest,
    Around midnight,
Remember that the sunshine,
    Is always on its way back to you.

1980's

If Only

What would we say to you now,
    If we could have you back?
What would we have shared with you,
    If you had not left us, too young, so long ago?

What thoughts would you share with us on me turning 30?
    For you would have been 36 this year,
Not forever turning 23.
    What answers would you have had,
For your nephews and nieces, for your little brother?

What stories you could have told them,
    And told your own children- if only.
If only you had not died,
    With your hopes, dreams and unborn children with you.

What would you have thought of the 'rents retiring,
    Bobby's new business,
Del's new job, my new life.
    So many things, if only.

If only we had you back for one day,
    To tell you how much we missed you,
To tell you how much we loved you,
    If only.

In a Million Years

You give me support,
        I give you dinner.
I give you support,
        You give me knitting needles.
It all works out in a million years.

And as I am there for you,
        You bring bagels.
As you are there for me,
        I bake cookies.
Who keeps track?

You may have sent more cards,
        I may have bought more roses,
When we are talking, you and me, who cares.
        We have at least a million years,
For it all to work out.

1987

The Death of a Million Years

The death of a million years,
    The end of a thousand dreams,
The beginning of a hundred tears,
    And letting go.

Sorting through countless memories
    Valuing, priceless moments,
Capturing the feeling of an infinite
    Amount of hugs

How many sharing joy,
    Or how many sharing sorrow,
No one will ever know
    But each one special.

Putting behind me,
    With much tenderness,
All that we were,
    To and for each other.

Dwelling no more,
    On all we had,
Plan to do,
    And letting go.

The Fool

I see a pathetic fool,
    Arms wrapped around himself,
Rocking back and forth,
    Uncontrollably weeping.

I see him grieve,
    In his loneliness,
Choking on his own,
    Self-contained feelings.

So much he should,
    Open his eyes,
And his arms,
    And let go of.

Instead of holding on,
    On the pain,
On the hurt,
    Like a security blanket.

It is amazing,
    I can even see,
This pathetic fool,
    Cry.

As he sits all alone,
    Rocking back and forth,
Crying out to empty walls,
    Of the pain.

And actually,
    I do not see the pathetic fool,
For there are no mirrors here,
    And the pathetic fool is me.

Jacqui's Story

The plane,
    Ascending,
The stomach,
    Descending.

Anxiousness freezes the moment,
    As an anticipation,
Makes it rush forward,
    To the moment of destiny.

Wind rushing by,
    Mocking my fears,
Opening doors
    Inviting my destructiveness.

Checking in
    Checking out,
Looking up-trying to check back in.
    Being pushed out

Fast fall,
    A moment - an eternity,
Eternity,
    In a moment.

Frozen,
    I could not pull the cord,
So it is pulled,
    For me.

And I float,
    Suspend in air,
Should I not have wings,
    For I feel like an angel.

Closer to God,

   Than I have ever been,
Feeling like I have found Heaven.
   And yet I am descending,
Is Heaven not up?

Soon, too soon,
   I landed
Already planning,
   My next flight.

www.ingramcontent.com/pod-product-compliance
Lightning Source LLC
LaVergne TN
LVHW041345080426
835512LV00006B/614